A Rendering of Soliloquies

Figures Painted in Spots of Time

Written and Illustrated by

Janet Kozachek

Finishing Line Press
Georgetown, Kentucky

A Rendering of Soliloquies

Figures Painted in Spots of Time

Copyright © 2022 by Janet Kozachek
ISBN 978-1-64662-775-2 First Edition
All rights reserved under International and Pan-American Copyright Conventions. No part of this book may be reproduced in any manner whatsoever without written permission from the publisher, except in the case of brief quotations embodied in critical articles and reviews.

ACKNOWLEDGMENTS

The poem, *First Step*, was published in the journal *Undefined*, Book Six. 2010 The poem, *The Standard*, was published in the journal *Ekphrasis*, Vol. 5, No. 1. Spring/Summer 2009. *The Pitchfork*, was published in *Local Life* Magazine, a publication of Hilton Head Island, SC, June, 2021.

I would like to thank all the people who took the time to sit for me, to sit with me, and to be by my side in the creation of this work. I am especially grateful to my husband, Nathaniel Wallace, for his support and encouragement, and to my friend Kristina Miller for preparing attractive PDF files for review. A thank you is also due to my sister, Jessie Thompson, for preparing book mock-ups in both printed and hand made formats. I am indebted to the galleries and exhibition venues from which many of the art works contained in this volume were collected, and to all my clients who have supported my life as an artist by investing in my art and in my writing.

Publisher: Leah Huete de Maines
Editor: Christen Kincaid
Cover Art: Janet Kozachek, Woman in a Red Shirt, Oil on Canvas, 9" x 9"
Author Photo: Nathaniel O. Wallace
Cover Design: Elizabeth Maines McCleavy

Order online: www.finishinglinepress.com
also available on amazon.com

Author inquiries and mail orders:
Finishing Line Press
P. O. Box 1626
Georgetown, Kentucky 40324
U. S. A.

Table of Contents

Introduction 1

Part One: Plagues

Introduction 5
First Step 7
Plagues 9
Woman in a Red Shirt... 11
The String of Pearls 13
The Red Stick... 15
Spring Buds 17
Salon Solitaire 19
White Cigarette Rising over a Ruby Glass............................... 21
Fat 23
Flat 25
On a Green Table.. 27
Purdah... 29
The Black Down Jacket 31
Mother Forgiveness of the Heart.. 33

Part Two: Gaming Songs

Introduction 37
Smokers in an Attic 39
The China Maiden.. 41
Word Play 42
Showering in the Ablative Case 43
Your Mother Has 45
Women of Dostoevsky.. 47
Games 49
Stichomythia 51
Contortion.. 53
The Staircase... 55
The Ballad of the Man in the Red Suit 57
Bacchanal... 61
The Letter... 63

Part Three: Journeys

Introduction 67
The White Dog.. 69
The Standard 71
The Red Thread... 73
The Yellow Dog... 75
The Quilt 77
Journeys 79

Elephant Ears Over Five Steps 81
Rose Bed 83
Song of Soup 84
Mango Bone 85
Hands 87
Diamonds in Serpent Eyes 89
Little Black Pot 91
Man with a Hoop 93
The Black Clock 95
Step Down 97
Good Wood 99
Morandi's House on the Hill 101
The Rose Familiar 103

Part Four: Celestial Beings and Lesser Gods
Introduction 107
The Green Cat 109
Celestial Beings and Lesser Gods 111
The Woman in the Chapel 113
Petroglyph 115
Man at an Organ 117
La Mente Malevola 119
Songs of the Kinnari 121
Café Bebe 123
Ostracon 125
Tall Bronze Woman 127
Double Blind Placebo Effect 129
Lauretta 131
To Dance with Gods 133

Part Five: The Mysteries
Introduction 137
Pentimento 139
Song Facing Inwards 141
Unremembered Dream 143
Pointed Shoes 145
Mysteries 146
The Horizontal Reading 149
Woman Before a Mirror 150
Dance With Fossil Fish 153
Red 155
The White Blanket 157
Any Man's City 159
A White Cat Comes In 161
The Pitchfork 163
The Empty Room 165

Introduction

In the mid to late 1990s, I painted a series of square paintings that I named *The Monologues*. The series was so named for the stories my models often told me about themselves as I painted them. With some exceptions, each painting featured a single person in an interior. In many cases the backgrounds were imagined or supplemented with architectural elements from other drawings. On occasions when models were not readily available, I used sketches composed of figurative details from old master paintings, classical sculpture, and some drawings of Renaissance sculpture.

Whether painting or drawing from statues or painting from live models, to keep the experience immediate, I generally eschewed photography. Painting and drawing from live models enabled me to listen as I painted. Some people communicated with dynamic gesticulations and colorful tale telling. Others were diffident, avoided eye contact and spoke only when prodded to do so. Creative people and scholars often read their books or engaged themselves in writing—defining themselves by their work and by being painfully conscious of wasting potentially productive time by just sitting.

I made written notes while the paintings were in progress, some of which became essays for exhibitions and for one publication. When I began to compile the paintings into a manuscript, it occurred to me that the relationship of language to the visual form would be best served by poetry. As I composed that first poem for the first painting, the words uttered by the people who sat for me returned to my memory, as did their stance, and their gestures. Their shared thoughts became the lexicon of my book. There was a poem for every painting, comprising five chapters: *Plagues, Gaming Songs, Journeys, Celestial Beings and Lesser Gods,* and *Mysteries*.

Over time, the relationship of the poetry to the paintings became quite fluid. Elements of some people's stories were attached to other people's images. Sometimes the poetry was more a reflection of my own experience than the people who sat for me. Eventually the figures became like emblems arranged with words, reminiscent of polysemous books from the Renaissance, in which the meaning of words and epigrams were simultaneously understood.

Some time after completing this book of poetry and paintings, I decided to make a black and white drawing version by revising and completing my preparatory sketches. I soon ran out of original material, as some canvases were painted directly from the model, without a preliminary sketch. Others were photographic composites. This presented me with both a dilemma and an opportunity. In order to fill in the missing paintings in a black and white drawing version of *A Rendering of Soliloquies*, I had to make new art works rather than just revise the older ones. This meant that my project took much longer than anticipated, but it also meant that I could create new illustrations that revisited the poetry with a fresh perspective. My drawings generally grew larger and more detailed than the original paintings. The dimensions also changed, as they ceased to adhere to the original square format. In some cases, I composed new poetry for the new drawings. The drawings became stylistically varied, with tightly rendered pencil patterns in some, and loosely integrated charcoal shapes and lines in others.

During the course of making drawings for the poetry, I came across an old photograph album from my father's World War Two service in the Mediterranean Campaign on the destroyer escort, The USS Wiffels. These photographs served as models for the poems, "Plagues," " Journeys," and "Mysteries." Regrettably, my father passed away in 2018, before I was able to publish the drawings and poetry that were inspired by his photography. I am at least content that I was able to share these drawings with him, if not the verse.

Eventually, I produced three versions of *A Rendering of Soliloquies:* the black and white version, the color version, and a mixture of the two. The present volume is a mixing of drawings and paintings. The work was so long in the making that some of the people who originally posed for me have advanced in age or passed on, and children have since grown. *A Rendering of Soliloquies* represents a protracted process of reflection and revision. Both the images and the poetry that these generated have been cultivated for over twenty-five years, all while smaller writing projects have been imagined, brought to fruition and launched. It is with gratitude and not a small bit of relief that this work has found a way to join completed works.

Part One:
Plagues

"He who plagues others, will be plagued himself."
—Zhuangzi

Introduction

To begin, I speak of plagues. I speak of plagues in the biblical sense of divine retribution for wrong-doing. I speak also of plagues in the literal sense of the horrors that may rain down upon us. I also speak of metaphorical plagues upon the spirit.

In the ritual of the Seder feast that I had the pleasure of partaking in, there was a custom of enumerating biblical plagues by dipping a finger in wine and flinging drops upon a cloth-covered table. A plague was shouted out with each drop that fell upon the table. "Locusts!" "Darkness!" "Boils!" "Frogs.!" In this ritual, these plagues were believed to be the divine means of deliverance from bondage. Yet the idea of enumerating plagues as a form of catharsis has surfaced in some modern Seder practices. In these, readily identifiable social maladies along with the traditional ones were also listed. The lists may include such things as poverty, war, hatred, sexism, racism—the banes that humanity needs to be purged of in order to proceed towards freedom and the pursuit of happiness.

Plagues are my poems about experiences and states of mind that cause discomfort. The written words cast them down upon the blank paper like the wine flung from a pointing finger onto a white table cloth. They shake out fear, confess jealousies, admit despair and loneliness.

The first poem of Plagues, aptly entitled "First Steps," is an amalgam of my conversations with two people, one who modeled for two of the Monologue painting series, another who related a story to me about a critical parent. The former person spoke to me about a mother so nit-picking that "she could make the Pope feel self-conscious." With that she began an amusing detailing of all the things she imagined her mother might say when confronting the Pontiff himself. Swinging her foot and lifting her head, she struck a judgmental tone with, "Are you really going to wear those shoes?" and "There's a stain on that vestment you know." Despite the sobering message, her soliloquy was hilarious. The second person's story upon which my poem was based related a similar tale of a perfectionist parent. Her tale was even more colorful because her experiences had seeped into the unconscious in the form of elaborate dreams. The dream she told me about was that of going into a room in her childhood house. In this room, she saw her mother bent over a child's footprint in paint on an otherwise clean carpet. The mother was mysteriously but frantically working over it with needle and thread. When asked what she was doing, the mother in the dream replied, "I'm embroidering over my child's first mistake."

The two women's words made their way directly into my first dispenser of plagues. Many others followed as my models related tales of their personal plagues: cast down in words, coloring language and image.

First Step (Woman Doing Embroidery), Pencil 12" x 9"

First Step

The child's painted foot presses the carpet.
Mother sets to work with needle and fine silk thread,
embroidering over her young one's first mistake.

Licking, sticking, finger pricking.
The mind of the hand that guides the needle
is stroking, joking, poking, choking.

The deed done, an imprint still remains.
In innocence it has no shame—
and even the pontiff's vestment can have a stain.

Sliding, gliding, threading a treading.
The eye of the needle fast upon the print
is staring, glaring, reputation scaring.

Permanence frightens to the core.
The paint that mother can't ignore
is set in baby steps upon the floor.

Hovering, smothering, errors covering.
The point of the needle over the mark
is nabbing, jabbing, wet cloth dabbing.

Stepping naively across the floor,
knowing not what paint is for,
the child leaves traces of where she's been before.

Gliding, striding, footprint hiding.
The stab of the needle over childhood tracks
is whipping, stitching, pleading, bleeding.

Plague, Charcoal and Pastel, 22.5" x 30"

Plagues

Child Plague
descends upon the unprotected
in her strung up bonnet and her buttoned down robe.
Helpless, vulnerable, incredulous,
the once confident, hale and healthy
fall like hollow toys before mindless fragments of biology—
little machines of codes that instruct to destruct.

Conqueror Plague
steps down upon the barren soil,
littered by the fallen, wiped clean of human touch.
Their once warm breaths are replaced by cold stillness.
Their once limpid eyes,
now stare blankly from desiccated sockets.

Immortal Plague
moves the life blood and flesh
from earth to sky.
Detritivores, in perfunctory duty
bring death to life again.
Carriers to carrion.
They carry on.

The Red Shirt, Oil on Canvas, 9" x 9"

Woman in a Red Shirt

There are lifestyles
that make it unnecessary
to wear pants around the house,
but to toss them casually over a doorway.
Draped like the paint on Rauschenberg's bed,
they hang over a head,
yet within an arm's reach.

There is a state of mind
that makes it not required
to close the window blinds at sundown,
or to take medications on time—
if one can find them
in an unlocked cabinet.

There is a time
when there is no concern
to count minutes, hours
days, weeks, months, and years
spent dripping into a divan—
ruminating on a box of tissues and an empty glass.

The String of Pearls, Oil on Panel, 10" x 10"

The String of Pearls

Between the prehensile thumb and the ductile fingers,
pearls roll back and forth,
 keeping time to her silent question,
"What was the meaning of it all?"
The question presses her brow into a narrow gorge
from which answers do not flow like rivers.

She tugs at the necklace,
turning it forward then backward.
She pulls it outward—
inviting solace to fall into the gulf
between her neck and the string of pearls.
"How could he have done it?"

This way, then that way.
The smooth cool white little balls
gleam around the irritant from which they were made—
that tiny seed of discontent
that time and layering turn into art.
"What had I done?"

Shifting and twisting upon itself,
the dewy spheres meet her searching fingertips.
She folds the string of pearls into the sign for infinity.
The necklace slips slowly from her grasp.
She lets it drop, and asks,
"Why me?"

The Red Stick, Charcoal, 12" x 9"

The Red Stick

He Brandishes a red stick.
With feet planted securely on the seat of a chair,
he creates a dichotomy
between fear and a safe haven
with his crimson line of demarcation.

Black cat and white cat
scurry restlessly on their side of the border.
They have claws that can scratch
and teeth that can puncture holes
in the skin of innocent babes.

A dizzying landscape
of vertigo verdant splendor
rises through the dependable railings.
An iron barrier holds back the kinetic foliage
from its wayward path.

Refusing to tread upon threatening ground
he retreats to his small square of immunity.
He plots his strategy there,
calculating carefully the distance
from his nemeses and the wait for their indifference.

Spring Buds, Pencil, 14" x 11"

Spring Buds

Lambent sunlight filters through open doors—
casting dense heads in aphotic shadows.
In fertile protected darkness the virus
of the red-eyed disease grows,
unseen but infecting everything.
On the caliginous side of a warm spring day,
eyes askance turn into
the classic face of envy,
obsessively following the course of goods withheld.
Staring into that insatiable abyss,
mouth pulled taught by thwarted desire,
she is a bitter witness to others' consummations.
Vexed at unshared happiness,
she ogles the crowning contentment
of her gratified rivals.
Their gardens thrive in verdant glory
under brighter suns.
Their flowering trees are heavier laden
with unfairly apportioned rain.
Boastful buds mock her misfortune,
barbed branches poke the embers of her eyes.

Salon Solitaire, Pencil, 12" x 9"

Salon Solitaire

Gatherers converge in animated conversation
on the subject of humanism and social alienation.
A wild flock chirps in existential commentaries
in the dim light of a café.

Her silent presence ruffles them.
They speak around and about her,
words circumnavigating the ribbons in her hair,
and circulating in meaningless sounds in her ears.

They do not speak her language,
and she is deaf to theirs.
The cadence of their voices rise and fall
in incomprehensible song.

Her feet planted firmly on the floor,
she does not yield her position.
The gatherers feast upon morsels of dialogue,
like birds pecking at seeds around the base of a tree.

Watching placidly as they disperse,
she touches her hand to her forehead.
She imagines a conversation over hot coffee,
the rising aroma carrying understanding to her consciousness.

Virginia Smoking, Pencil and Charcoal, 10" x 8"

White Cigarette Rising Over a Ruby Glass

Two companions inhabit a late night room:
tobacco rolled in opaque white paper
and red wine in a translucent glass.
They serve as sustenance for a second and third shift,
and the blessed means of sleep
in an impromptu space called home.
Home. A place to temporarily close one's eyes—
shutting out the diaphanous glaze
of a hastily hung drape.
Street lights peer inquisitively
through the spaces between weakly woven threads,
making a shadow puppet of the soul that dwells within.
The late late late show, short hours before the dawn
features a puff on a cigarette.
She swallows from the red elixir of blinking and nodding
as the little room rattles from passing trucks
and a police siren splits the night air.
A belligerent voice howls out—
the screech owl of the urban forest.
"AAAAAAAAAAh!"
"Who you lookin at!"
I said, "Who you *lookin* at!"
Sounds of the city, its cries are muffled by alcohol,
like a wad of cotton blunting a knife blade.
In subdued increments of drowsy exhaustion
her heavy lids meet in the middle of the road
that stops at the smallest fragment of the day.
Fourth shift. Sleep.

Man with a Glass, Pencil, 14" x 11"

Fat

There is the problem of your weight—
that bulge falling over your belt,
like so much ice cream in the cones
your father bought for you,
and for which you paid.

There is the trouble of your voluminous flesh—
expanding from your chin
like the swelling throat of a bull frog
singing for his mate—
one that you cannot find.

There is the conundrum of your corpulent self—
round little soccer ball
from the gym class of your youth—
where you waited and waited.
You were the last one to be chosen.

There is the predicament of glossy lean bodies
that smile tauntingly from the magazine rack
across from the cartons of candy bars,
that tug your eyes with temptation
and cast spells upon your belly.

There is that frustration of fat
acquired with ease from
the cherry coca cola in your glass,
irrigating the adipose rolls that stay and stay
like the unwanted guest that never leaves.

Julia Resting, Oil on Canvas, 9" x 9"

Flat

In her search for level ground
a crevice appears.
She rakes the crumbled earth lightly
to fill it.
But it will not be filled.
Like the furrows of tilled land,
it remains open to receive its seeds.

In her quest for an even plain
a ridge appears.
She works it over with her hands
to make it uniform.
But it will not become planate.
Like the undulations in desert sands
it reappears with the changing wind.

In her hunt for the flat land
a knob appears.
She grooms it out with a fine tooth comb
to straighten it.
But it will not straighten.
Like the curls in her baby dog's fur
it will not unfurl.

In her longing for a smooth finish
a wrinkle appears.
She presses it down with her iron tools
to flatten it.
But it will not flatten.
Like the striations in the bark of her ancient oak,
it deepens as it grows.

Mask Room, Pencil, 12" x 9"

On a Green Table

The verdant cushioned couch
stretches out ahead,
like a velvet upholstered tarmac
laying out a pathway
for airborne homunculi to land.

A green table pulls forward
to guide the way backwards
to a point that vanishes
in the heart of a young boy,
who stares through the lenses of over-sized glasses.

The blue granite stove
opens its mouth,
disgorging its bounty of paper works
onto the receiving table—
a conglomeration of unread books
and rolled up plans.

There are promises delayed
in those unsigned documents.
Dreams cut short
in those unfinished books.
Unworn masks hang upon
Sedona earth walls,
keeping silent vigil over paths not taken.

Woman Among Shadows, Charcoal, 12" x 9"

Purdah

Seeing but unseen,
she absorbs the light—
like so many colors
that turn to grey
upon her polygon dress.

Hearing but not speaking,
she clasps her fingers together—
like so many angles
that cancel each other out
on the yellow of a curvilinear chair.

The silent listener
grows with cast down lights—
like so many shadows on the wall
enlarged beyond the pale tin wafers
of their cut out forms.

Feeling but not felt,
she presses her silver
slippered feet together—
like so many mute stones
that touch the corners of a space.

Knowing but not known,
she knits together her brows—
like so many Madonnas
sequestered in a crypt—
gazing through the gauze of their veils.

Woman in a Black Down Jacket, Charcoal, 14" x 11"

The Black Down Jacket

Obsession floats like warm bloated air
between a body and a black down jacket,
cushioned against air that stings
and light that shines too brightly.
An inner set of buttons, an outer set of snaps
fasten together in a layer of knotted laces.
Outer pockets hold alcohol swabs
neatly sealed in foil packets.
These converge with inner pockets
of plastic wrapped raisin filled scones—
a sanitary feast to partake of
just in case of minor calamities and major inconveniences.

A cool zephyr passes her upraised nostrils
that sniff around the room for
evidence of leaks,
gas not turned off,
fans that perchance still run
unmonitored, unsafe.
Clouded glasses turn the eye's vigilance inwards.
From stained glass roundels
set in pairs in a corner room,
She sees a duality,
counting the polarity of serenity and discontent
like gold and tin coins,
one against the other.

Anxiety lies in the secret recesses
that are stuffed with hidden keys,
looking for safety behind locked doors,
zippered containers and sealed vaults.

A compulsion rises to set things straight
when eyes align with a zig-zag room—
or when a stool sits with one leg
not quite reaching the floor.
It wobbles between weightlessness and the ground—
tipping away from that elusive solidity of rest.

Mother Forgiveness of the Heart, Oil on Canvas, 12" x 12"

Mother Forgiveness of the Heart

Sister Pain of the Body
curls up in a wicker chair,
daring not to touch her feather weight feet
upon the cool, hard bricks of a patio floor.
Gravity pulls hard against that which hurts.

Daughter Fortress of the Vigilant Brain
shields soft interiors
from biting winds and armies that invade.
Intrusions scar deep into that which is laid bare.

Protector of the Threshold
snaps alert and upright,
like the eyes and ears
of her little black dog at attention.
Sickness overcomes those who are unwary.

Mother Forgiveness of the Heart
gently releases a softly flowing stream.
Mercy meanders along the turns of a poking past,
its soothing water nourishing all in equanimity.

Part Two:
Gaming Songs

"I'm afraid that sometimes you'll play lonely games, too. Games you can't win 'cause you'll play against you."

—Theodore Geisel, *Oh, The Places You'll Go.*

Introduction

Stories, games, and songs have the uncanny power to profoundly shift a focus, and in so doing, return a temporary sense of humanity to the fearful through the language of wit and with the cadence of music. In Boccaccio's Decameron, for instance, a motley group of souls sequester themselves away in the countryside in order to hide from the plague-infested cities. To amuse themselves they tell humorous stories that serve to distract their attention from the terror sweeping the country and snatching the lives of their fellow human beings.

The poetry in part two of *A Rendering of Soliloquies* consists of songs, word play, and riddles. The inspiration for these playful rhymes come from a number of sources: Chinese antithetical couplets, the poetry of ancient Greece, jazz and blues lyrics. The poem *China Maiden,* for instance is a pun on "made in China," a label that dominates contemporary commerce. The entire poem is an adventurous rollick through a number of Chinese characters that incorporate the element of woman into their structures.

The poetry of *Plagues* were the verses of cries. The laughter of *Gaming Songs* counterbalances these cries. Laughter, however, is not always lighthearted mirth, just as cries may not always signify anguish. Some of the poetry of Games is darkly sardonic and told with a hint of sarcasm. *Smokers in an Attic*, for example, was based upon a sign in an actual attic in Germany that forbade smoking. Nothing says forbidden with as much force as the German word *verboten*. The following songs are not forbidden, however, and instead irreverently invite a collective smirk, or serve as musical cautionary tales.

Smokers, Charcoal, 12" x 9"

Smokers in an Attic

Forbidden acts in hidden spaces
were the kind that Adriaen saw—
among strewn papers and stacked book cases
against an attic wall.

City dwellers in a Bohemian town
were the ones that Adriaen knew.
The miasmic vapors settled down
as their raucous laughter grew.

Policing calls and siren strains
were the sounds that Adriaen heard.
Sweet succor flowed throughout their veins
as they whispered their secret words.

Guiltless paradise beneath a cloak
covered the souls that Adriaen sought.
In a dark corner, puffs of smoke
Embraced them in their loft.

Zuth in a Red Jacket with Plum Blossoms, Pencil 12" x 9"

The China Maiden

The China Maiden enters with a bow.
She stands upright and center.
Her fingers grasp the world
and her red jacket proclaims joy.

She climbs out of water and earth.
Ascending gracefully up a mountain,
she pretends to be a fairy or a sprite,
flying high among the clouds.

With one companion she is shaman.
Alone she would have been a Buddhist nun,
if not for her girlish ways
and a horse sense too keen for monastic life.

The China Maiden is matron of the crossbow.
Yet she relinquishes the game she fells in wild grass,
retiring instead to a vegetarian repast.
She finds herself in the midst of foolish rambling for it.

The excellent China Maiden
wipes the sweat from her comely brow.
Her strong hands knead dough
quietly, at peace beneath her roof.

Word Play

There is a door,
that is a door
that Isadore adores.
Until a door ration,
for a duration,
brought her adoration
to the floor.

Dancing Maenad at a Door, Pencil, 8.5" x 11"

Showering in the Ablative Case

Strips of patterns stand in conjugated rows
like the cases of a Latin noun.
They alter in morphology as they decline.
Nominative green and blue stand at the forefront.
Genitive possesses the golden brown earth—
in warm juxtaposition to red Dative.
A penultimate verdant column, accusative,
draws the line between exterior and interior.
Ablative poses the last barrier to the vulnerable nakedness of a showering man,
standing alone in his niche.
As striking as a Roman statue affixed to a pedestal,
he wipes the age off his body with a red towel.
Man, a noun in the ablative case.

Showering in the Ablative Case, Pencil, 7" x 5"

Your Mother Has a Million Eyes, Charcoal and Pastel on Paper, 26" x 20"

Your Mother Has

Your mother has a billion fingernails,
that click and clack upon your back.
Your mother has a hundred earlobes,
that swing and cling to pretty things.
Your mother has a million eyes,
that peer in fear when danger nears.
Your mother has ten thousand wrists,
that twist and turn for your concern.
Your mother has a thousand eyebrows,
that twitch and knit when shoes don't fit.
Your mother has a hundred elbows,
that prod and poke unruly folk.
Your mother has a dozen nostrils,
that sniff and flare for fetid air.
Your mother has a pair of lips
that are red and beg for your forehead.

Women of Dostoevsky, Pencil, 9" x 12"

Women of Dostoevsky

The fallen child of Niobe
melts bonelessly over a promontory of earth,
like Salavdore Dali's immortal clocks,
painted in the heat of the night.

A red-faced man smiles in furtive delight
hiding the power of the holy Roman emperor in Kyiv,
as he officiates over the women of Dostoevsky,
caught in a perilous embrace.

The spinner of tales and the weaver of lace,
bound by lips of blood and red pepper vodka,
kiss with a lacerating beauty
—cannibals of each other's lusts.

The dark maternal ancestor of Pushkin trusts
that sage pinwheels will always turn on golden sand.
Her blue and brown stalwart body
stands chiseled out of a cold winter day

Games, Charcoal, 9" x 12"

Games

Girls play games.
Women do the same.
They skip rope, use soap,
and they don't say "dame."

Girls smell a rose.
Women selected and chose.
They play cards, plant a yard,
and they paint their toes.

Girls laugh high.
Women will sigh.
They motor boat, tie a float,
and they jump from the sky.

Girls start small.
Women grow tall.
They ping pong, sing a song,
and they read the law.

Girls play ball.
Women sit in Town Hall.
They shoot skeet, wash a sheet,
and they use a chain saw.

Girls eyes shine sun.
Women make mascara run.
They ice skate, start out a gate,
and put a lock on a gun.

Girls peek and peep.
Women collect and keep.
They run around about town,
and then they go to sleep.

Woman and Hydrangeas, Charcoal and Pastel, 25.5" x 19.5"

Stichomythia

I watch the tossing of your head.
My head knows many secrets.
Does your tongue long to tell them?
Only with your notice that I possess them.

I see you in the twist of the buckle on your shoe.
My shoes have walked through many towns.
Do your feet ache to enter the doors you find there?
Only when I know that you will follow me.

I notice the reflections of blue upon your brow.
It is nothing more than blue from the hydrangeas in a vase.
Do you long for the gardens from which they were plucked?
Only when you unlock the iron gate and welcome me inside.

I watch the clouds of violet above your eyes.
My eyes have seen such beautiful things.
Does your heart beat faster when you look upon them?
Only when I know they can be shared with you.

I observe a blush of pink across your cheek.
It is merely the pink from a picture of plum blossoms on a wall.
Do you wish to sleep beneath the tree from which they fell?
Only when I know that you will awaken with me there.

Contortion, Charcoal and Pastel, 19.75" x 23"

Contortion

She felt life through ivory skin,
and perceived it with sapphire eyes.
She created a world from a refuse bin,
then compressed it to bantam size.

She moved in contortions to twisted rhymes,
in a dance of corporeal sense.
In musical voice she sang sanguine words,
which had no future tense.

Her fingers spread beyond eight keys—
Chopin was never hard.
She did parlor tricks with flexible ease
in the comfort of her back yard.

She had no god but believed in dreams,
thinking neither of heaven nor hell.
Yet she worshiped the sunlight on tannic streams
and drank from an artisan's well.

The Staircase, Charcoal and Pastel, 12" x 9"

The Staircase

The stairs went up
and the stairs came down,
with no way to come in
or go out on the town.

The men danced up
and they leap-frogged down.
With heels over head
they spun around and around.

The children ran up
and they tumbled on down,
in their striped bow ties
and their Buster Browns.

The ladies stepped up
and they sashayed down,
glittering as they went
in their satin evening gowns.

Tap tap tap ta ta tap tap tap
sisha choo sisha choo sisha bang bang bang bang!

She walked up the steps,
then she tip toed down.
She hummed a funny tune
and then danced like a clown.

She tapped out a rhythm
but got tired of the beat.
So she sat the bottom,
last step at her feet.

Bah baba bah baba bah bah bah
bong bong bong bong. STOP!

Man in a Red Suit, Oil on Panel, 12" x 12"

The Ballad of the Man in the Red Suit

Walking through the woods at night,
gliding through the dark,
don't tug upon his red suit
or make his hunting dog bark
—because he knows your terror
like a shark knows blood.

His smile deftly hides a knife,
when he encourages some sharing,
as he talks about his wife
and your sympathetic caring
—because he feels your desire
like a shark feels blood.

Don't paint your face for him
when your heart fills up with need.
Consequences will be grim
when he calculates your greed
—because he smells your lust
like a shark smells blood.

Don't let him know that you have dreams,
or what you long to do.
With him its just a fishing game
with bait and hooks for you.
—because he can hear your yearning
like a shark hears blood.

Don't let him see your wounds,
or where you used to bleed.
Don't tell him of your sorrows,
or he'll come up to feed
—because he senses pain
like a shark senses blood.

He's not the one to lean on
although he tempts you to.
He is the lean and mean one
with an appetite for you
—because he tastes your weakness
like a shark tastes blood.

He moves silently across a room
when all your friends are loud,
glaring in affected gloom
within that joyful crowd
—because he sees that you have secrets
like a shark sees blood.

Don't cry or tell him why
you find the world a threat.
He singles out the shy
for his private tete-a-tete.
He'll feast upon your tears
like a shark feasts on blood.

He'll speak with tenderness.
Don't leave a space for him to fill.
Don't accept his sweet caress.
It means he's ready for the kill
—because he knows your longing
like a shark longs for blood.

You can feel his eyes upon you.
He casts a shadow on your face.
When he draws you towards him,
bow down and whisper grace
—because he's moving closer
like a shark gets close to blood.

Bacchanal, Oil on Canvas, 9" x 9"

Bacchanal

Pan cried out to Billy and Harry
from his forest apothecary,
"I'm mixing herbs for both of you.
Come drink them down and when we're through
we'll have fine wine and boisterous song,
with elixirs and potions mixed thick and strong."

The two men laughed and got their flasks,
pulled on tight pants and donned their masks.
With beastly horns and feathers of fowl
they set off for their Bacchanal.
They frolicked in the woods like naughty satyrs
in lascivious scenes on Grecian kraters.

They danced to the river with running and leaping
and grinned at a nymph as she lay sleeping.

Then stealthily they started creeping,
to hide behind a rock from which to be peeping.
With sniggering mouths and teary eyes brimming,
they smiled at a Silenus who was there swimming.

They took his clothes just for some fun
from where they were drying out in the sun,
and hung them high up in the trees,
then tied his undergarments around their knees.
From off the bank they took his hat
and played with it from where they sat.

Then gleefully through the forest they ran.
And when at last they greeted Pan,
they gave him gold and talked nonsense.
Pan filled their flasks in recompense,
and served them comestibles beyond measure
for the rest of their evening of foolish pleasure.

The Letter, Oil on Canvas, 9" x 9"

The Letter

The analog woman in a digital age
wields a pen in her hand on a postmodern page.
With Victorian manners in a room of her own,
she has strawberries with tea and jam on a scone.
On Sunday morning at a window in the early spring light,
she savors her fruit with the most incremental of bites.
Pining for sisters long gone and friends fully grown,
with ink flowing like blood she writes out her tome.

She types postings, reports and logs about dangers,
in an anonymous corner in a web full of strangers.
But only one pair of eyes sees the words from her pen
—nineteenth century verse written over again.
On a table adorned with pansies and thistle,
she unburdens herself in that tiny epistle.
She then folds it neatly inside a tinted green casing
and binds it with glue and with words self-effacing.

Part Three: Journeys

"When in April the sweet showers fall. And pierce the drought of March to the root, and all. The veins are bathed in liquor of such power. As brings about the engendering of the flower, when also Zephyrus with his sweet breath Exhales an air in every grove and heath Upon the tender shoots and the young sun His half-course in the sign of the Ram has run, And the small fowl are making melody That sleep away the night with open eye. So nature pricks them and their heart engages. Then people long to go on pilgrimages. And palmers long to seek the stranger stands Of far-off saints, hallowed in sundry lands."

—Geoffrey Chaucer *The Canterbury Tales*

Introduction

A journey begins when the familiar is left behind. The familiar can be a physical place or a state of mind. It can be microcosmic, like the molecules of genes that journey through generations in the poem *Elephant Ears over Five Steps*. Or the familiar can be written large, as in *Journeys*. The poetry in this chapter concerns itself with a breaking away from the comforts of what is close and familiar through forays into new vistas and novel places.

The models for these paintings were people, sometimes with their animal companions, who have traveled in one way or another. Their journeys were sometimes an exploration of a collective past through objects, as in the poem and painting *The Little Black Pot,* written for the grand-daughter and great grand-son of Maria Martinez. The ceramic objects referenced in the poem literally traveled from one generation to another, polished by the oils from successive hands.

Some of the poetry of *Journeys* represents personal creative searches. *The Red Thread*, for instance, is structured around a German phrase, *der rote Faden des Erzhalen*, which my philosopher model described in terms of his individual search for meaning and continuity in his journey through the world of ideas. Other poems were inspired by those who ruminated upon their physical aging, while those with young, lithe and wiry bodies expressed excitement for their journeys ahead.

The White Dog, Oil on Canvas, 9" x 9"

The White Dog

She returns from a journey,
cloaked in white fur,
as a robe she wears
when cloistered from the outside world.

She remains hidden from herself,
and from a truth that curdles on her tongue
like a bitter herb
that makes her mute.

She growls softly through her white fur,
soiled by a muddy roll of dice
played by God and the universe.
Double fives on white cubes.

She speaks in numbered voices,
counting and dividing hopes by regrets,
whimpering softly to closed eyes
and a head resting upon a sturdy fist.

A white dog searches
through her dewy eyes.
Begging for a bone of absolution,
she tugs at a white skirt,
worn for protection against the scratching paw.

The Standard, Charcoal and Pastel, 12" x 9"

The Standard

A marble torso of a man,
his face turned dispassionately sideways,
stretches out to the limits of his human measurements.

As fingers graze impenetrable boundaries,
he hovers like a protective muse.
He is the keeper of life spans and increments of sure footing.

He is steady, cautious,
moving step by step,
wary of the indigo embers beneath the surface path.

A burning blue passion
beats eternally against the edges of allotted space—
sounds that only yearning and innocence can hear.

The Red Thread, Oil on Canvas, 9" x 9"

The Red Thread

Baffled before the armoire
and not knowing what to wear,
he crouches naked on the floor
to search for a red thread.

A red thread that binds
umbilical cord to mother,
or spirals upward and outward,
like a ribbon dancer's gift to her anonymous spectators.

A thread that could weave his unruly love
into sensible tweed,
or a thread free to meander like a vine
that clings to the roots and the stems it feeds upon.

A red thread to carry his aspirations,
like veins that carry his life blood.
Or messages upon a wire,
like nervous impulses conducting themselves across a synapse.

A thread plucked
like the straight taut string of a lute,
or inextricably jumbled,
like the saffron noodles intertwined in a bowl.

A red thread that braids together
rows of parallel impressions—
influences that tug against the heart,
sinuous lines that wheedle sense from chaos.

The Yellow Dog, Pencil, 12" x 9

The Yellow Dog

The yellow dog lies lazily across a patterned carpet.
He finds contentment in designs from ancient Rome.
By turning one ear he catches sounds behind his back.
Enthusiasm bubbles from a child,
who cavorts with her curly-haired mongrel.
Does she know that the Carolina yellow dog
preserves the DNA of ancient companions to First Peoples of America?
Is she aware that he is truly an antediluvian breed,
who made the voyage across the Bering Strait
when the ice age bound America to Asia?
Perhaps not.
What she knows is that his journeys are now marked
by the edges of patterns in a room,
from carpet to tile to upholstery to wallpaper.
Oceans away and far from the ancestral home,
the yellow dog rises,
taking his primordial blood to the kitchen for a scrap of food.

The Quilt, Pencil, 14" x 11"

The Quilt

Woman sufferer rises
to the occasion of bearing children—
or bearing not to.
Her body, as earth's instrument,
yields to ground
yet surges with the tides.

Woman transcendent sits aloft
in her blue cotton dress.
She plans for work and waits for play.
She creates strategies for the survival
of herself and her troops,
drawing a battle line in marching triangles.

Woman triumphant stitches a quilt
within the confines of snatched moments,
when the young sleep and men need nothing.
She pieces together the fabric of their histories,
fastening the fascinating geometry of a worn through past.

Port in Sicily, 1944, (after Walter Kozachek Sr.) Charcoal, 22.5" x 30"

Journeys

Where do men's journey's take them?
Into ports where others clamor about them.
Curious onlookers cluster around,
some scowling, some beseeching,
some wanting to see more.
Others do not wish to be seen.
Some are barely there.
They keep their distance, in their ghostly presences—
like the one-legged man who watches cautiously from afar.

Where do journeys take men?
To places where barefoot children
climb upon the wheels of a carriage,
their agile feet entwined between the spokes.
Their smudged faces smiling with unknown intents.
Intrepid explorers in ragged clothes,
their hunger making them bold.

What takes men on journeys?
The cries that emanate from across the seas?
Or the songs that lead them down narrow passageways?
Voices from the other sides of closed doors?
Or faces that beckon from beneath arched windows?

Why do men journey?
To escape the ordinary.
Search for the extraordinary.
To gaze upon unfamiliar faces.
To hear unknown voices,
and to find them the same as those from home.

Elephant Ears Over Five Steps, Oil on Canvas, 8" x 8"

Elephant Ears Over Five Steps

Five steps serve as couriers of messages:
adenosine, cytosine, guanine, thymine and uracil.
Is it destiny or is it possibility,
that calls our molecules to order
in the same chain of command
that our ancestors marched to?

That pure Purine and pyrimidine.
Is it fate or is it inclination,
that circulates in the blood,
ringing the same bells that
tolled for those who went before?
Poor purine and pyrimidine!

Guided by building blocks like steps in a great garden,
tracing a path beneath elephant ears and caladium—
Is it written in stone or an impression upon the earth,
smoothed over by the upper hand of lifestyle and serendipity?
Your uracil remembers still.

The double bind of the double helix.
Is it a sentence or just a warning?
Secret codes permeate the living flesh,
beating the same drums our forebears gyrated to
as they danced in blessed ignorance of their genes.

Pebelle, Pencil, 14" x 11"

The Rose Bed

A coverlet of pink and red
lies draped across an ancient bed.
Folds cascade down softly,
like the fallen petals of roses
in an autumn garden.

Rose bed—
where life began
in a bath of exuberant vermillion.

Rose bed—
where secret pleasures were first known
and shared in intimate bonds.

Rose bed—
on which the sick convalesced
and the weary body slept.

Rose bed—
where the meandering mind dreamed
of exotic places and worlds both frightening and sublime.

Rose bed—
whose sweet pink folds of warmth
absorbed the tears of pain,
providing succor for the pangs of rejection
and absolution from the guilt of refusals.

Rose bed—
her velveteen softness offered her bounty of respite,
soothing fuzziness where life began,
was lived, then carried away.

Song of Soup

Blocks of concrete stood in industrial rows.
Laundry hung limply off the line,
paraphernalia strewn along the grey balconies
poured out from the cornucopia of cramped apartments.

The remains of the Soviet block
served as dingy camouflage for the folkways within.
A woman sang native songs
in peasant frills donned inside a worker's walls.

Bucolic melodies rang crisp and clear
as notes fell into a tin pail alongside peeled carrots.
Pointing in chaotic directions,
sharp orange soldiers made their way to peasant soup.

Tanya Singing, Pencil, 12" x 9"

Mango Bone

You cannot avoid her sitting there,
watching you from her place near the doorway.
She greets you in her Jamaican lilt
on your rite of passage to the kitchen,
where a warm sun-drenched chair awaits.

You cannot miss her waiting there,
in her overflowing body
draped in a generous gown of flowers
printed on white chemise—
growing and withering with her steady breath.

She wants to tell you of her mother,
the one who worshiped the mango bone.
The mango bone was exposed by a ritual knife
that penetrated the stiff and reddened skin
and carved out the sweet and golden flesh.

She wants to tell you of her grandmother's patience,
as she listened to song birds from her back porch,
all the while scraping the chunks of fruit from the clinging pit—
every last fiber peeled down to the bone.

Carol Reclining, Charcoal, 8.5" x 11"

Artist's Father, Oil on Canvas, 9" x 9"

Hands

Hands like rafts
floated upon an ocean
of time and endurance.
Years worked strength into fingers
like wind and rain upon timbers.

Hands of labor
created foundations and structures.
Framed by muscle, bones and duty,
a knuckle was sacrificed for every member
who lived within these walls.

Hands grasped
tools, boards and companions
to do right by.
When sinews bent no more
and bones grew thin with wear,
he framed the empty architecture
in the hollows of his palms.

Ruth with Artifacts, Pencil, 9" x 12"

Diamonds in Serpent Eyes

On her perch as citizen of the world,
nestled among the silks of old Arabia,
a woman languished in the soft luxury of precious textiles.
Sprays from the Amazon encircled her head.

Harlequin tiles were set at her feet—
redolent of the Papal splendors of Avignon.
Glassy cold squares decorated with beasts and fowl
circumnavigated their gold and green world
in lines of pedestrian brown.

She recalled her childhood
and summer days spent on the banks of sacred pools,
where warm nights brought bejeweled snakes
from the boughs of trees
and out of the still waters of a collective unconscious.

The serpents came not to feed but to inform,
belly dancing through the reeds and rushes.
They glided by with diamonds in their eyes,
faceted jewels that caught the sunlight,
and dispersed it to the six harmonies of the earth.

The serpents wound their way close to her heart,
not to frighten but to reassure.
They wrapped themselves to make a mandala
around the warmth of stones,
coiling around with their supple splendor.

They slithered in sigmoid curves,
knowing of her dreams for wisdom,
their eyes sparkling with reptilian awareness.
They heeled at her feet.
They healed at her feet.

Man at a Fair, Pencil, 9" x 12"

Little Black Pot

Little black pot was smoothed into being
by hands warmed in the sweat of the sun.
Generation upon generation
folded their earthen coils,
molded them onto hollow clay,
and shaped them into vessels that held the breath of their ancestors.

Makers of bowls, these clever ones,
pressed them into existence by hands made expansive by what they held.
Creators of twin jars,
made them howl with the waters
that flowed in passages between them.

Parched lips touched red earth
polished by round stones
that once tumbled in the bellies of dinosaurs
as they lumbered across the land
in their Mesozoic journeys.

The sojourn of the spirit
scratched out in a white line,
meandered across the black and brown clouds,
and hovered over a burned piece of cloth.
It traced a path around and around
the world of a polished vessel.

Daughter to daughter and son to son,
hands rubbed their essences onto clay.
Oils of the flesh eased its way into the little black pots.
These pots survived
—blackened by smoke and fire which consumed the air
beneath a nest of gnarled branches and the dung of beasts.
Hands caressed surfaces that soothed the heart
and wiped away the sting of feeling less than
yet being more than, a little black pot.

Man with a Hoop, Pencil, 14" x 11"

Man With a Hoop

A green rectangle,
golden in its architectonic purity,
holds a circle.
A round pool of sky
is set in a patch of sod-covered earth.
Ferns beckon with frilly fingers,
barely grazing the boundaries
of roundness against squareness.

A tall man makes a tondo
of running legs and hips,
brown against earthen yellows and emerald greens.
He sees a porthole to free-wheeling times
in schools for alternative education,
where he learned to sleep while standing up.
He holds his hoop in a somnolent hand,
keeping a steady foot upon the base,
while dreaming of Renoir.

The Black Clock, Charcoal, 12" x 9"

The Black Clock

A black clock hangs demurely on the wall,
her round moon eyes staring out of her hour glass shape.
Wooden cogs turn metal hands
on a shorter arm and a longer arm,
pedantic seconds tugging at their shirt sleeves.

An empty rocking chair rests against the wooden floor
—a toy for a child's make-believe home.
A girl counts the spaces in between it's spokes,
the useful and the useless.

She steps into a room with high stocking feet,
gingerly holding a bit of lint
plucked from the blue woven carpet on the floor.

The little flaming square of window sends out a spark
to her ghostly green dress,
and burns a glint of light onto a vase of dried flowers.

The piece of lint she holds sends her imagination beating backwards
curious as to it's travels on shoes both strange and familiar.

Step Down, Pencil, 11" x 14"

Step Down

On a short journey to a sub floor level,
a young girl pauses on two steps.
Her slight smile and averted glance
hides an awareness of being watched,
as if even the walls have eyes.

Grasping knees to chest to hold in a moment,
she listens for a sound as her cat silently sleeps.
Her ears catch the long sonorous notes
of a distant viola, which rise suddenly
and swiftly in shortened staccato notes.

A bow bounces along viola strings
like a bird on a hot wire,
stumbling upwards in a crescendo of sound,
that youthful ears find exciting.

In her young imagination,
a vial of oil, a violet, and a viola
hop scotch together
like three sisters close in age.
She, the youngest, plays the longest,
last to step down, cross a room,
and step out.

Good Wood, Oil on Canvas, 8" x 8"

Good Wood

The black and white
of being and non-being
stand juxtaposed
in flesh by seasoned wood.
Good wood reclaims chapters
of living, loving, longing
scrounging a bit,
and making do.

A Day of the Dead soul seat
watches with hollow eyes,
grinning with his painted on wit.
He heaves a sigh
from a crooked breast
and hips tilted in contrapposto
that the restless find unsettling.

Good wood makes things right
by ferreting out the art
in salvaged stuff.
Finding purpose in a balancing act,
chairs stand on two legs, three legs, then four.
Truncated, trussed up, and trusted,
their painted, glued and reassembled
old history yields to new tales.

Morandi's House on the Hill, Charcoal, 12" x 9"

Morandi's House on the Hill

It was summer in sun-drenched Tuscany.
A farmhouse stood rust ready
against a turquoise sky—
a colossus looming darkly
from the crest of a hill.

In the valley below
trees stood in manicured rows.
Aligned like the soldiers of the Roman legion,
they prepared their advance
to a space beyond the picture plane,
bringing the Pax Romana
into the uncharted territory of a livingroom.

A woman waited there patiently, dreamily,
dressed in white with red polka dots.
Her form was silhouetted against the sunlight
that cast shadows long and broad in the late afternoon.
A patch of cerulean blue from Morandi's hillside
fell onto her earlobe,
pretending now to be a jewel.
The sun shone out from that far and away place
and struck the green forest of her carpet,
where her heliotropic feet rested
against a frosted sundial of a throw rug,
delicately poised to invite Morandi home.

Julia in the Hibiscus Garden, Charcoal, 12"x 9"

The Rose Familiar

A melange of floral grandeur
eases into a radiant noon,
its pink and white largesse blossoming
like the enamels
on a Chinese porcelain vase.
It is the rose familiar
to embroidered waistcoats
of eighteenth century gentlemen.

She steps forward as if to walk,
yet pauses to test the ground
in a garden path between
leaves of lemon grass
and nodding hibiscus.
They stake a claim upon
love and possession
in their bountiful excesses.

Turning,
then returning,
at the end of his tether,
her little dog looks backwards.
His canine eyes track the distance
between his violet pink ribbon
and vistas unbounded.

Part Four:
Celestial Beings and Lesser Gods

"Hail, children of Zeus! Grant lovely song and celebrate the holy race of the deathless gods who are for ever, Those that were born of Earth and Starry Heaven and gloomy Night and them that briny Sea did rear."
 —*Theogony*, Hesiod

Introduction

Celestial Beings and Lesser Gods opens with a departure from the usual motif of a single person in an interior, for the only living presence in this room is a cat. The poem is based upon a Chinese myth as it was told to me by a French diplomat. In this myth, heaven decides to open its gates to allow the animal kingdom in. All the animals of the world eagerly scampered, flew, or crawled into paradise. The only animal that did not proceed was the cat, who decided that he was not interested in entering heaven on that particular day. Although not wanting to be bothered to proceed through an open door seems especially characteristic of a cat, the diplomat, who was also a Chinese scholar, explained that the cat's diffidence was an allegory of the human social order. The cat, he explained, was a symbol for the independent-minded artist, intellectual, or poet.

This poet, like the cat, leaves the answers to questions about the existence of God up to the reader, wishing neither to meet with the divine, nor make any judgement or guide to belief. The poetry of *Celestial Beings and Lesser Gods* nevertheless dances with the notion of immortals and otherworldly beliefs. The imagery in this section comes from sources in both eastern and western mythology and in both ancient and modern art. The gods can be malevolent, as in *"La Mente Malevola,"* or beneficent, as in "To Dance with Gods."

The Green Cat, Charcoal, 8" x 10"

The Green Cat

Golden gates open to paradise,
inviting animal souls to enter.
In beckoning light
and comforting warmth,
the windows on the divine
cast their glow upon the earth.
Gods on high shine down upon them,
making a first,
then a second request
for their gracious company.
Heaven opens to all beasts
of burden and obedience.
Accompanied by ethereal voices,
they tread, they fly,
and they scurry in.
Everyone, except for Cat
who thought paradise not for him.

Celestial Beings and Lesser Gods, Charcoal, 12" x 9"

Celestial Beings and Lesser Gods

Objects upon a white cloth
lay as offerings to people passing by
in the torpor of late afternoon shadows.
A solitary apple, a tempting trinket,
sit as the trappings of yearning
for a warm bed and respite from hunger.

A mass of woman sits
swaddled in a woven coat
and a thinking hat.
She nods her head downwards,
as hypnogogic hallucinations
fly within and without the hollows of trees.

Celestial beings and lesser gods,
half human and half chicken,
turn right side up and upside down
in their flight between somnolence and wakefulness.
They have been conjured.
They cavort among the boughs,
and then are exorcized
from haunted limbs.

Woman in a Chapel, Charcoal and Pastel, 9" x 12"

The Woman in the Chapel

Beseeching arms stretch outward,
reaching fruitlessly for Adonis.
A love unrequited
stirs her aching heart.
With his body striding forward
and his gaze turning back,
a smile of tenuous empathy,
or a self congratulatory grin,
filters across his face.

He sees a woman in the chapel,
a silhouette against the fleeting light.
She sits in nebulous shadows,
like a mirage upon the marble floor.
Her face thrusts forward in bold pursuit,
her nose guides the way towards
an invisible yearning.
Yet the image on the stone wall remains frozen.
So too, does the smile on his face
—cool, proud object of a goddess's desire.

Petroglyph, Oil on Canvas, 9" x 9"

Petroglyph

Under the scrutiny of an Asian mystic,
an uncarved block
yields it numinous secrets.
Roving over the undulations and interstices of stone,
his mind's eye carves magic beasts;
a snake against a sigmoid curve,
a bear around a bulge,
a bird with an arched neck feeding its young,
and a lizard in a labyrinth.

At last the mystic applies his chisel to the rock face,
bringing form and shape to his imagination.
The carved block yields to the purpose of the tool
that follows the machinations of the mind.
Resting from his labor, he prepares himself some tea.
Serving it up to the goddess of the moon.
He hopes that for eternity,
she sees the visions made manifest in rocks.

Man at an Organ, Oil on Canvas, 9" x 9"

Man at an Organ

Organ sounds rise and reverberate
across green painted pews
and through indigo balustrades.
The organist's white hair
illuminates his face like a halo.
He closes his eyes to the notes upon the page,
preferring instead the pure,
tactile sensation of resonating keys
and the slow giving of pedals
pressed underfoot.

The cool blue chapel offers respite
from a summer afternoon in Lombardia.
Music fills the chambers,
beating a sound against the stained glass
and echoing inside the domed ceiling.
A mosaic icon stares out from underneath an arch,
its tesserae catching the fleeting light of late afternoon.
Drops of gold swirl in waves of andamento,
like notes strung together in rhythmic sound.

La Mente Malevola, Oil on Canvas, 9" x 9"

La Mente Malevola

The Spanish professor, with his ebony black curls,
sank his aching bony body deep into his hostess' living room couch.
"I don't believe in God," he said,
inhaling the capital "G" off the word.
It sounded odd.
"But," he warned, "I do believe in *La Mente Malevola*."
"He plays with us you know," He said,
while waving his hand back and forth in the air.
His obsidian Rasputin eyes glowing with malevolent irony, he went on,
"Like the cat plays with his mouse before killing it."
I laugh out loud at what I believe to be the utter facetiousness of this confession.
But an image is emblazoned on my mind
—the visage of *La Mente Malevola*, the malicious mind.
La Mente Malevola, an evil force in the universe,
grinning down at the vulnerable,
like a rapacious cat beholding his impuissant prey.

How could anyone believe in such a god? I ask.
A god with nothing better to do than intervene in the lives of men?
Why should a *Mente Malevola* even bother to waste god time
playing cat games with worthless mortals? I wonder.
It seemed as ludicrous as believing in guardian angels
—silliness at either end of the metaphysical poles, I think.

Then a three-day migraine visits my wondering brain
with searing light and sickening sound.
That familiar thudding beat in my head
was something like...
Batting back and forth...
Like the cat that plays with a mouse before killing it.
La Mente Malevola stared down upon me
from his perch in the cosmos,
his feline eyes gleaming with cruel desire.
And I believed in a mind of malicious intent.
I believe. *I believe in La Mente Malevola.*

Man Attacked by Birds, Charcoal, 7" x 5"

Songs of the Kinnari

Melodious calls of women-headed birds
abound in an Indian paradise.
Mellifluous songs resonate from their lips.
Their breasts, round like ripened fruits
flow with the succor of milk and honey.

A man of Greco-Roman bent
looks upon the Kinnari with fear in his heart
and loathing in his mind.
Mistaking them for harpies, he closes his eyes
and presses his hands against his ears.

The Kinnari perch upon popagay feet,
their toes painted rose like those
of women who frequent salons.
Their bejeweled feet are beauteous
wrapped around with leaves of gold.

Too terrified to look skyward,
Greco-Roman man runs deaf and blind
from the assaults in his imagination.
In his mind's eye he sees tearing claws
ready to rip his body
like the frenzied Bacchantes
who tore the flesh of Pentheus.

The songs of the Kinnari ring
in Indian heaven,
as music of the spheres from creatures
half woman, half bird and wholly divine,
elevating those who listen to celestial music.

The man, still running,
dares not stop to catch his breath.
In his mind's ears he hears harpies,
their tongues like stinging whips
ready to lacerate his tender heart.

Café Bebe, Oil on Canvas, 9" x 9"

Café Bebe

A hundred bathing cherubim
splash in a mountain stream.
Their shining piglet bodies bounce about
in otherworldly emerald green waters.
Their downy white feathers flutter
on rolls of baby fat.
Like winged hams on a picnic outing,
they tumble in Teutonic dreams.

A vision of infants dance
on top of the head of a red faced drinker of spirits.
He reaches toward a laughing lady
to end the light on a cigarette.
A glowing hot ember is snuffed out—
like a genie prevented from granting a wish,
and instead turned back into smoke in a bottle.

He deliberately crushes the fiery butt,
tapping out a code with it against a fluted glass tray.
TAP TAP, TAP TAP TAP
—like the march of gaily clad foot soldiers
who smile through the lines
of their polished white teeth
while singing Heimat music
carried by an Alpine breeze.

Mysterious Mr. Repoussoir
looms black against the corner stall.
The Halloween lantern suspended from the ceiling
swings on its haunted link chain.
The mirror reflects in its iron frame,
the visage of a refracted babe.
Split down and across his center line,
he bends double over a glass of blue wine.

The Ostracon, Pencil, 12" x 9"

The Ostracon

A golden glazed urn once held precious oil,
poured out by a priest in small decantations.
Suppliants watched a drip ease its way
down the buff and pink bodied terra cotta,
turning amber, then green.
The overflow was sanguine warmth to them.
The largesse of the giving vessel
quenched their thirst for the holy.

Sun to sun and moon to moon,
a sacred trust was sealed by oil.
Seeking wisdom, initiates were anointed
by priestly oil-daubed fingers
that gently touched their lamenting chests.
He greased their brows to assuage their sorrows
and massaged holy oil into their beckoning hands.

Aged and worn with use,
Time dulled the once shining urn,
chipped its sacred feet, and split its curved body.
The priest, acknowledging its uselessness as a vessel,
smashed what remained in the most perfunctory fashion.

A shard found its way into mortar in a road,
treaded upon by pilgrims to ancient shrines.
The rest became ostracons
—purveyors of notes written in coal and ink
upon the porous inner surface.
The words curved ever so slightly inwards.

Scattered pieces withstood their time in the earth,
until archaeologists pulled their remains from the dust
in order to read their cryptic, fragmentary notes
about two bags of flax sold, justice for a stolen calf,
and the day that three liters of oil were purchased for the temple vessel.

Tall Bronze Woman, Charcoal, 12" x 9"

Tall Bronze Woman

The tall bronze woman
stands pulled, peeled and frozen.
Her fingerless lumps of hands
are welded fast to her naked body
—a form that stretches
to meet Giacometti on high.

Duchamp lies ready made
in the red purgatory of a painted wooden cage.
His dead pan bed pan witlessly swings
in white enameled irreverence from a string.

In the middle ground,
a gesture makes a right handed "Y",
In the foreground, a sign leans into
a backhanded compliment.
A counter points to paper works floating
in an earthly pool on a mirror covered desk,
like water lilies in a nebulous Monet,
split between what is read and what is real.

Double Blind Placebo Effect, Oil on Canvas, 9" x 9"

Double Blind Placebo Effect

A man borrowed from a parade of pilgrims
enters a small chapel,
cool with stones and worn with rocky relief.
He kneels down, raising both arms,
and clasping his hands together.
He closes his eyes in firm resolution
to pray before empty orange chairs.
Passers by chuckle to themselves
at his blindly fervent devotion to missing authorities.
They keep their bemusement quiet,
as these chambers carry magnified sound.

This man does not know if his saviors are present
or if they are not.
But his faith in their existence is held up
like the suspenders that grasp his pants,
suspending doubt, so that eyes need not open.
He can smell the scent of votive candles.
Having faith in a benevolent presence,
he is saved by a grace beyond unoccupied seats,
like the missing medicine that should be there
but heals nevertheless with it's double blind placebo effect.

Woman at an Art Fair, Pencil, 9" x 12"

Lauretta

A puff of tree
springs from malachite fingernails,
growing off a raised hand
like the metamorphosis of Daphne.
The reaching hand
hails a distant acropolis,
faux finished
in mock grandeur.
Gems rest there,
gilded like her millifiori dress,
awaiting patiently
the mercantile grasp.
A ziggurat of crimson hair
spins off her head,
a conscience framed by poplars.

Apollo like,
we creep behind
—our faces in the darkness,
searching for jewels
to grasp and call our own.

The Temple of Eternal Joy, Oil on Canvas, 9" x 9"

To Dance with Gods

She cast down an empty hand
—a hand no partner clasped to dance.
Waiting to be asked was a tiresome thing.
Her joy remained in just one upturned foot
that sought to capture the toe tapping rhythms
and the heart beat of bass strings.

The hand not proffered
made her recall times among Tantric sculptures
hidden in Buddhist grottoes.
They silently signed with their fingers
in that temple of joy
—inviting an embrace
with their plenitude of arms.

Monks chanted in low bass notes
in a cave that magnified the sound
and sent it curling,
sensuously hugging the stone walls.
Deep music caressed skin with sound,
until the notion of fleshly self dissipated
and dying was to dance with gods.

Part Five:
The Mysteries

"The most beautiful thing one can experience is the mysterious. It is the source of all true art and science"
  —Albert Einstein

Introduction

The images and poetry in this chapter are about the unfathomable: hidden secrets, and unanswerable questions. In the poem/image, "Pentimento," for instance, these hidden items shine tantalizingly through to the surface, as if longing to be freed. In other poems/images, the unknown lies implied in spaces beyond the picture plane.

Many of the people who sat for my paintings and drawings in this volume were people who pondered metaphysical questions, like the philosopher who wrote about aesthetics, or the woman who often found herself ruminating on questions of philosophy and religion. There were subjects who chose mysterious professions, like the woman who became a psychologist in the painting "Red."

Mysteries, and this collections of images and poems, concludes with "The Empty Room," positing the riddle of whether this emptiness signifies an expectation of a future with human inhabitants, or documents their permanent departure.

Pentimento, Charcoal, 14" x 11"

Pentimento

In a foundation of a painting,
there was a barren room.
In a second layer of pigment
stood an occupant
—a woman who invited the artist
into the interior.
The artist observed
that she turned her gaze away
as the woman became a man.

Time transformed paint
into diaphanous veils of color.
The ghosts of a previous sex,
a smile, a look,
then a room shone through.
Like a photo luminescent creature
from the depths of a primordial sea,
its translucent jelly membrane
displayed its inner workings.
A forethought was born again
in *pentimento*
—the artist's transparent repent.

Man Playing a Flute For His Cat, Oil on Canvas 9" x 9"

Song Facing Inwards

The music is purest
from behind the head,
beyond the gaze of questioning eyes
and detached from working lips.

The melody sounds truest
from beneath the fingers,
playing in columns of air
that spoken words cannot grasp.

The memory rings clearest
from behind the face,
considering its reflection
that shines out from the looking glass.

The rhythm beats deepest
from within the heart
catching the last rest note
that falls from a half step not taken.

Sleeping Man, Charcoal, 14" x 11"

The Unremembered Dream

Slumber falls like dark blue clouds
on a moonlit marine.
Sliver light plays
across his face
like a lunar sheen.

Awakening,
the essence of an unremembered dream
lingers in the air,
like the musky perfume
of a departed lover
—gone—yet the scent remains.

Pointed Shoes, Charcoal, 12" x 8.5"

Pointed Shoes

Tiny feet with pointed toes
graced with pointed shoes.
Jewels of the lotus
pressed inside
red silk upon red soles.

A purple robe,
a backwards chair
in a blue room where beatniks roamed.
Manhattan memories of
golden skin
with only leaves to wear.

Mysteries

A woman launders,
the cool water splashing against her strong thick hands
that knead a soaked garment.
Like a boneless sea creature tossed up from the deep,
the wet cloth yields beneath her grasp to expel a liquid breath.

Pressing, turning, and pressing again,
the laundress' hands force unwanted soil
slowly out towards the waiting waters.
She pushes, wrings, then flips a shirt over
in an exorcism of stains.

The laundress stares out and away
from her manual labors.
What mysteries of thought reside behind her gaze?
What hidden past is sequestered there?
What uncertain future captures her mind's eye?

Bending over her washing,
the laundress labors on.
She presses the soil of the past
into a clear and present pool of water
—water of mirrors reflecting timbers
turned serpentine by gentle waves.

A storm of human imagination
built with complex molecules of suds,
whirls upon the cistern.
Was this conjured, perhaps,
by an indulgence in spirits from a bottle
that temporarily eclipses sense and sensibility?

What secrets hover above a ladder
that ends before a horizon begins?
What strangeness lurks
in the blackness of an open door?
Dirt, carried away by water

that tumbles down a ledge never tells,
nor confesses to its origins
as it slips into the water,
cascading over ancient blocks of stone.

Women Washing (after Walter Kozachek Sr.), Charcoal, 28" x 22"

Horizontal Reading, Oil on Canvas, 9" x 9"

The Horizontal Reading

A long shadow of late afternoon
yawns before her,
like the mystery in an alley
on a DeChirico canvas.
The dark line on the blue horizon
reading from classical left to Biblical right,
shifts along a straight and narrow path.
Fleeting light mingles with the stars
sprinkled like the milky way on her spotted dress.

The yellow sun of a brilliant day
opens its eyes before her,
like spotlights on a stage
that follows spinning young dancers.
Ascending light draws a reader up a page
from Mesopotamia below to the Orient above.
Flowers blossom from behind the pages of a book
and reach for tessellated words in stone.

Woman Before a Mirror

A reflection of a brown-haired daughter sits
poised on the threshold of re-invention.
She wonders how new wings will feel
as she flies away from past duplicities.
She listens for the distant wail of a train whistle
—a plaintive cry that tugs at nostalgia.

The brown-haired daughter
folds the blue drapery in her smooth hands.
The velvet evokes a memory
of being cradled in strong maternal arms.
She yearns to know a life withheld
but is mindful not to mourn omissions.
She forges ahead instead to new uncertainties
that lie beyond the edge of a looking glass.

A brown-haired daughter pretends
to be in control of her destiny
in the self-actualized
transcendental American way
of pulled up bootstraps and esteemed resilience.

She finds there is no peace there
—only a community of the lonely
sequestered beyond transparent borders.
She touches the glass wall that divides
one from the other,
fretting that they will be deaf
to each other's cries across immutable boundaries.

The brown-haired daughter taps
cautiously upon the silver glass
that separates reflection from the corporeal,
seeking a place where inside and outside converge.

The future is a confounded mystery,
eluding intentions and expectations,

mocking both dreams and apprehensions
from the watery realm
of its looking glass world.
The brown-haired daughter calls fate down
to either open its flood gates
or slither beneath a doorway.
She is ready.
She is waiting.
She is fit to take a great unknowing leap,
to attempt a landing upon a spot unknown.
Unafraid of death but fearing pain,
she hopes that landing will not bruise her fledgling soul.
Yet fly she will.

Woman at a Mirror, Oil on Canvas, 10" x 10"

Dance with Fossil Fish, Charcoal and Pastel, 11" x 14"

Dance with Fossil Fish

She dances in grey and black
while grasping fossil fish
—their primitive scales interlocking
like the armor of a silver knight.

They wear their coats of mail
to guard their brackish flesh
from gourmet palettes
—despite their uselessness to the taste.

In a parody of joy,
the dancer's dark companion leaps too,
wishing also to live
beyond featureless silhouettes.

For the sister that glides in the light
her shadow brother moves in dreams and memories
—brothers that wear their male coats
of the Dance D'amour in the cold of a silver night.

Darah, Oil on Canvas, 9" x 9"

Red

Like Lady Lazarus,
she rises from the ashes,
the embers of her hair glowing
from the puffing of lovers' breath.
Her curls coil off her head,
flowing downward
like crimson spirals of Mayan sacrifices
unfurling in a stone crypt.

Red locks burn
against the ice blue of her starry eyes
and sear a hand against a foot.
They bathe the room
in hues of exuberant sunrise
on clouds of red, red, red.

The White Blanket, Pencil, 14" x 11"

The White Blanket

An exclamation point of hair
springs from her head
like a shocking revelation
that sprouts from seeds sown long ago.
What was once unseen, is now known,
birthed from the head, fully grown.

A white blanket grasped by one alone
is chosen from a nest of woven fibers,
fertile with patterns,
copious in tactile complexities.
But it is the plain white downy blanket
that she clasps close to the softness of her skin.

The white blanket comforts,
shielding with an apotropaic warmth
against the cold specter of adulthood,
too soon to bear down upon the unprepared
as she tests the waters of an outside world
with her one foot dressed in a frilly cuffed sock.

Any Man's City, Oil on Canvas, 9" x 9"

Any Man's City

In a land of literary imaginings
there were grand bridges, noble arches
and warm stucco towers,
stained by earthen red and yellow ochers.
Silver leaves of olive trees rose off curling branches
from rocky pastures dotted with painted goats.

White horses bowed their heads by the emerald green river
that ran by the old city on the hill.
It was a place without time.
It was nowhere and any man's city,
arising out of the need for a context to a story.

Unfolding on a thespian's stage,
the painted backdrop of a place
for a teller of tales was there because…
He must be from somewhere.
The place must be about something.

The actor sat there waiting like one half
of a pair of star-crossed lovers.
He perhaps fancied himself a master mind
of intricate political plots
and fragile, dangerous alliances.
Or perhaps he was the bard himself,
crafting a drama and imagining
how it would play out
when painted upon the perceptions of an audience.

A White Cat Comes In, Oil on Panel, 10" x 10"

A White Cat Comes In

A calculus of squares and triangles bound within and without a hoop
overflowed into a flat land of geometric patterns.
Blue seeped into white and a sprinkling of white settled onto blue
—like snow on a distant mountain.
Geese flew by in red along a meandering periphery,
marking the ends of territories.
A white cat sauntered in,
altering the balance of borderline divisions in a square space.
The artist gazed upon his feline presence,
as he tucked his little arms beneath his delicate body.
White folded onto blue as pink blossomed into white,
like rosy spring lips that kissed the silver hairs of winter.

Woman and a Pitchfork, Charcoal, 12" x 9"

The Pitchfork

June arrives at a back porch
where labor rests
and the sun dances,
circling in confusion
on the stucco side of a yellow home.
Nearly forgetting what labor brings,
a woman of a certain age sits
barefoot upon cement steps.
She stares silently upon a yard,
espying weeds to pull
hedges to trim,
and cracks in cement to fill.
Setting out to fill her day by counting down tasks,
she tasks herself instead
with watching the play of sunlight
that coquettishly appears, then disappears,
as she flirts with the concept
of a guiltless joy at doing nothing.
Just for a moment,
the pitchfork resting by her side,
pierces the mutable light.
It's utility stands in counterpoint
to an unearthed desire to grow
in graceful twists of uselessness
like the aging trees of Taoist sages.

The Empty Room, Charcoal, 12" x 9"

The Empty Room

There was an empty room
with all but light removed.
The old timbers rose darkly as shadows
against the white-washed plaster.
There were walls that held echoes
in a solitary sanctified parcel
of unadulterated space.

An unoccupied domain
enticed like nirvana
—nothing dying, nothing born.
In that quiet peace of void
there was a simple pleasing stillness,
like a soft exhalation.
The silent domain
held the mystery of unanswerable questions:
Have all souls departed?
Or have they yet to arrive?

Janet Kozachek hails from Princeton Junction, New Jersey, where her rural formative years were spent drawing and writing in nature. Her subsequent education was unusually eclectic, having traveled, worked and studied in Europe, China and the United States. Her Master of Fine Arts Degree in Drawing and Painting is from Parsons School of Design in New York, where she also studied poetry with J.D. McClatchy. Her Certificate of Graduate Study in Chinese Art from the Central Academy of Fine Art (CAFA) in the People's Republic of China included the study of Chinese poetry and painting. Her undergraduate study at Rutgers was in science (biology) and art.

In addition to her painting, Janet Kozachek is a well-known mosaic artist, and was the Founding President of the Society of American Mosaic Artists. Her work is in a number of museums and private collections, and she was the recipient of the award for excellence in drawing from Art Fields (2019), a Puffin Foundation Award, National Endowment for the Arts awards, a Heritage Foundation Award, and a Humanities Council Award. Her poetry and illustrations have been published in *Undefined* magazine, the journal *Ekphrasis*, and *Local Life*. Ms. Kozachek is the author of ***The Book of Marvelous Cats***, an illustrated book of rhymes for the cat, and *My Women, My Monsters*, an illustrated chapbook of poetry. *My Women My Monsters,* won an Honorable Mention award from Concrete Wolf Press and was published in 2020 by Finishing Line Press. Janet Kozachek was the recipient of the 2020 Common Ground on the Hill Award for Excellence in the Traditional Arts.

When not writing, drawing, or painting in her studio in Orangeburg, South Carolina, Janet Kozachek finds joy in cooking, gardening, and handcrafting ceramic musical instruments.
Ms. Kozachek is represented by the Artisan's Center in Walterboro, SC.
www.janetkozachek.net
www.kozachekart.blogspot.com
kozachek@bellsouth.net

www.ingramcontent.com/pod-product-compliance
Lightning Source LLC
Chambersburg PA
CBHW040306170426
43194CB00022B/2921